ACCESSING GOD-
THE EVOLUTION OF ENLIGHTENMENT

FROM KUNDALINI YOGA
TO
5-MEO-DMT...
THE KEY TO ETERNITY

by
Lewis Sanders

ACCESSING GOD-
THE EVOLUTION OF ENLIGHTENMENT
FROM KUNDALINI YOGA
TO
5-MEO-DMT...
THE KEY TO ETERNITY

Sanders, Lewis   ACCESSING GOD-
THE EVOLUTION OF ENLIGHTENMENT
FROM KUNDALINI YOGA
TO
5-MEO-DMT...
THE KEY TO ETERNITY

ISBN # 978-0-9980237-1-7

1). Modes of Illumination
2). Advanced Yoga Theory- Kundalini Yoga
3). Psychedelic Yoga- 5-MEO-DMT DPT DET
4). Entheogens

Eternity Blue Productions
Literary Distillations of Lysergic Proportions

Printed in the United States of America

10 9 8 7 6 5 4 3 2

Cover photos are of the hand-cast belt buckle given to the author in 1969.

This book is dedicated to the fine lifetime work done in the field of higher consciousness research & reaching God by-

Albert Hoffman, Bernard Aaronson, Aldous Huxley, Blas Pablo Reko, Myron Stolaroff, Richard Evans Schultes, Valentina & Gordon Wasson, Houston Smith, Oscar Janiger, Peter Furst, James Arthur, Sasha & Ann Shulgin, John Beresford, Michael Hollingshead, Timothy Leary, Robert & Ester Lowe, Michael Horowitz, Peter Stafford, Jonathon Ott, Rick Doblin, Ralph Metzner, David Soloman, Lester Grinspoon, Stanislav Grof, Bernard Roseman, George Andrews, Thomas Roberts, Rick Strassman, Roman Hanis, Jack Adams IV, Augustus Owsley Stanley III, Nick Sands, Tim Scully, Darrell Lemaire, Casey Hardison, George Harrison, Robert Forte, Hamilton Morris, Philip Dick, Ken Kesey, Terence McKenna, Dennis McKenna, Roy Buchanan, Sir John Woodruffe, W.Y. Evans-Wentz, Glen Bernard, Theos Bernard, Sri Aurobindo, Swami Satchidananda, Dhyanyogi Madhusudandasji, Swami Dharmananda,
... & of course, for all of you yet to come.
See you There

This book is the end result of over 30 years of personal research into The Divine. What I have learned is simple. There are certain God-given ways for those of us down here to access the next world and if properly followed, these paths will lead you directly to God. From there you're on your own. Don't worry tho'... for this is what you're here for. To find God & resolve life's mysteries. But you must make the first move.
God won't come to you until you take the first steps.
Whatever path you choose...

ACCESSING GOD- THE EVOLUTION OF ENLIGHTENMENT

This is a test. A test to see if you can transcend this world of Illusion, get through the maze, and find God. If you do, you will find Heaven & a Life beyond your finest dreams. If you don't, you will be stuck in the material plane amidst its evil forces, temporal joys, & myriad of sufferings until you do. However many lifetimes it takes in this world. And this world and evil itself will last only until the final Earthly Soul achieves Enlightenment and rejoins The Whole.

Only then will our human mission be complete.

Good Luck and don't look back...

ACCESSING GOD-

THE EVOLUTION OF ENLIGHTENMENT

FROM KUNDALINI YOGA
TO
5-MEO-DMT...
THE KEY TO ETERNITY

CHAPTER 1

Throughout the Ages there have been several God-given paths to human Enlightenment; i.e. the direct revelation of the Divine Source and nature of our Being. Found usually only by those inquisitive Souls who knew enough to be looking. Looking for the hidden Secrets of Olympus, the Door to the Immortals, & the Eternal Kingdom of Terrapin. That which seemingly lies beyond both ends of this life and not amidst the middle.

These secret Mysteries of Antiquity were discreetly handed down to hand-picked initiates who spent decades in preparation for this knowledge & honor. Whether they be Gnostics, Egyptian Mystics, Shamans, Alchemists, Heads of Eleusis, or Buddhists of High Tibet, their quest was always the same. The Quest of the Golden Stairs, looking for the Secret of the Golden Flower. (Opening the Thousand-petaled Lotus to the Inner-Sun within.) That is the ability of the human being, or Soul, to leave the material plane and traverse the Divine Realms of God.

The numerous recorded instances of people throughout history whom naturally, (through devotion, prayer, and meditation), or spontaneously, (by the grace of God), have experienced this Mystical State have been the main source of knowledge of the Heavenly Realm available to the general public up until now. Books such as Cosmic Consciousness, by R. M. Bucke, 1901, have documented the wondrous few such as William Blake, Dante, Walt Whitman, & Francis Bacon whom attained the Godstate and great insight through Transcendental Union with God.

1

Those people who have "clinically died" temporarily and returned to this plane, provide another source of reliable reports of the immense beauty and allure of the next world and our next state of existence.

That this experience of Divine Enlightenment is an innate possibility within each & every one of us is the true secret of our Being, and the full realization of the Highest purpose of the human form. If the opportunity that this extends to humankind was completely comprehended for what it was, it would make the greed & petty wars of mankind vastly minuscule in comparison.

Through Yoga, (which means *Union* in the ancient Sanskrit language), this knowledge has been distilled into an exact science of Soul-release; in which the practitioner separates their Soul from their body, and briefly returns to the Heavenly realm of God as God's guest, to ascertain true existence.

So Yoga then, is an ancient God-given process by which one may safely induce "clinical death," meet God, experience Heaven, & then return to this world. This is a process which involves both the physical & the metaphysical worlds. The practitioner must use both the physical body and the etheric body; which is not physical at all, but is an energy body, much akin to the human nervous system. Through concentration and imagination, both may be harnessed and utilized for the activation and movement of the usually dormant Soul.

Although through the system of Buddhism this knowledge had been traditionally recognized as Truth in the East; it was not until the early 20th century that such brilliant minds as Sir John Woodruffe- (Tantra of the Great Liberation 1913, Serpent Power 1919); W. Y. Evans-Wentz- (The Tibetan Book of the Dead 1927, Tibetan Yoga & Secret Doctrines 1935, & The Tibetan Book of the Great Liberation 1954); and Theos Bernard- (Heaven Lies Within Us 1939, Hatha Yoga 1943); sought out, translated, & returned to the West with knowledge of this Supreme Spiritual Process. From this intellectual migration came an expanded understanding of the life-defining system of karma, the re-incarnary nature of our existence, and the true purpose of our Earthly Trip- finding our way back to God.

This system of Yoga then, can briefly be described as follows: that in our normal waking state our Soul, (called in the ancient Vedic Sanskrit language *Kundalini*, or coiled serpent), lies like a sleeping snake coiled 3 1/2 times around the base of the spine, guarding the Door to Eternity. Through the ancient Yogic techniques of visualization, breath control, concentration, & willpower, the Soul is awoken; and with the further application of concentration, breath control (*pranayama*), & yogic body locks (*bandhas*), the Soul is then moved into and up the spinal column, into the head, and out of the body.

Once awakened the Kundalini rises up through the central canal of the spine, (the *Sushumna*), drawn by the yogin's intense concentration & visualization, and propelled by the yogic body locks and the release of

3

cerebro-spinal fluids within the spine... (one of which is the chemical key to Higher Consciousness). Upon reaching the throat level, (the 5th of 7 energy vortexes or *chakras* in the body which the Soul passes through on Its journey up the spine & out the body), the now awakened Soul or *Kundalini Energy* then passes into the 6th chakra (the *Pituitary Gland* or *Third Eye*) in the middle of the forehead. Here the Soul merges with Consciousness, and more of the higher consciousness chemical is secreted which facilitates the passage of the Soul onward. From the *Third Eye*, the Soul moves across the top of the head (the *Rainbow Bridge*), into the 7th chakra (the *Pineal Gland*) in the center of the head, & then exits the body through the soft spot at the back-top of the head. (The *Fontanel.*)

Once the Soul departs & joins God, the body will remain in an entranced state of suspended animation for as long as the Yogin has oxygen stored within their system through *pranayama* to support their "sleeping" physical being. Then when the stored breath has diminished, the Soul naturally returns to the body, the Yogin regains consciousness, and this Earthly world once again becomes, (or stands in as), the primary objective reality. Though one now knows for sure that Reality lies far outside of this world and far beyond the bounds of breath...

Since the early 20th century then, the knowledge of Yogic physiology, (the *etheric body* or energy body, the *nadis-* energy currents or veins which run throughout the etheric body, the *chakras,* & *Kundalini*), has been available to both the East & West, and many have gone

4

that route with great success. In the mid-late 20th century, these Yogic truths began to be verified through "Scientific discovery". Kirlian photography revealed the aura and the etheric body. Einstein & Quantum Physics revealed that all matter is truly but a dance of vibrating energy- energy that can neither be created nor destroyed, and is thus eternal.

Which in turn is the very nature of God- Pure, Blissful, Eternal, Divine, Energy-Consciousness.

God is pure energy & the Godstate is a non-material state of unitive, ecstatic, electric thought... one of true, loving intellect, and one orgasmically psychedelic in nature...
God is Pure Vibrating Love.

As it is a non-ordinary state of consciousness, to attain this Godstate it is necessary to alter one's normal state of consciousness and raise one's vibratory rate to gain access to the Higher World. Yoga does this very precisely through the afore-mentioned techniques. There are other manners in which to alter your consciousness and attain this state of Grace. Traditional alternative methods such as the dancing of the whirling Dervishes, extensive fasting, sleep deprivation, self-flagellation, & the like (The Sun Dance) all depend upon stressing the human body to the extreme point of releasing the Soul. This is not particularly good for the physical body; (which actually should be viewed as The Temple of the Soul and treated accordingly), which is why the Yogic system was devised by God and handed down through-out antiquity.

5

The main drawback with the Yogic system is that if the initiate has not properly prepared their body through Hatha Yoga and the stretching of the spine over time, then serious damage to the mind & nervous system could occur when the Kundalini Energy awakens and rises.

When the Kundalini travels up the spine it is like a million volts of current going through your normal house wiring. The spine must be strengthened to handle the load. Also there are 3 psychic energy blocks which lie along the spine, (lower abdomen, navel area, & throat), and these must be overcome through committed practice of the *bandhas* or body locks, or the awakened Energy could get stuck along the way and cause unwanted physical and mental aggravations. *Once again, one must be properly prepared, stretched out to the max, and thoroughly know the complete techniques of liberation before one attempts any awakening of the Soul through Yogic means.* In reality this is not a drawback at all, but it's a safeguard for the Higher World. A danger exists only for those who would storm the gates of Heaven unprepared and without proper intent. Foolishness and impatience never bring Enlightenment- only danger and trouble. Heed the warning, respectfully prepare, and God will welcome you Home.

That's all that this life is truly for.
A cosmic unveiling of Existence by God to us all,
one by one.

CHAPTER 2

Although the basic Yogic technique, vehicle, and Spiritual opportunity have remained unchanged for thousands of years, newer aids to & modes of Enlightenment have been made available to us by God over time. And for good reason.

Although the evolution in scientific knowledge in the 20th century Western culture revealed a closer understanding of the true reality behind our world, other scientific developments sought to annihilate this advance in perception altogether. The advent of the nuclear bomb & nuclear power brought the specter of planetary death closer to Earth than we'd ever known before. To make up for this, a Swiss sage would unknowingly discover the antidote to human stupidity and Spiritual depravation- LSD.

In 1943 the honorable Dr. Albert Hoffman, a Swiss chemist working for Sandoz Ltd., discovered the Spiritual/Psychedelic properties of *lysergic acid diethylamide,* which he had been the first to synthesize five years before. LSD was undoubtedly given to the world by God at this point in time to counteract the sheer insanity which humankind was subjecting itself and the planet to. And in the 75 yrs. since, LSD has had a most profound effect on millions upon millions of people- opening them up Spiritually & intellectually beyond all non-entheogenic* sacraments before it.

Peyote & hallucinogenic mushrooms had been providing Spiritual insight and communiqué for native populations in Mexico and elsewhere for millennia. Other societies had more complex entheogens, made

7

from the roots and bark of trees and vines in the jungles of South & Central America. LSD however, made the psychedelic-religious experience available in a flash; giving the world, and especially errant Western society, a major tool of discovery denied it up until then.

LSD, like these other hallucinogens, served to reconnect the human Spirit with nature & with God. One could firsthand learn from the plant kingdom about the Divine inter-connectedness of all beings in and with The Cosmos. Likewise the re-discovery of the use of psilocybin mushrooms in Mexico in 1955 by R. Gordon Wasson, ensured that wider knowledge of their existence and use would continue for untold ages. These psychedelic discoveries in the 1940's & 50's led to whole generations of young people in the 1960's, 70's, 80's, 90's, and into the 21st century & beyond; who actively used psychedelics to explore & expand their consciousness with Spiritual intent and unlimited expectations. And among this group, the classic Mystical Experience began to happen more often; leading to a resurgence of interest in God, the Yogic path, & Eastern mysticism which continues today.

That's because rightly used, psychedelics tune you into The Spirit and The Spiritual World like nothing else. Embodied in these Sacred plants lies all of the wisdom of God, contained in a form to ingeniously impart this Knowledge to humankind. And from this expanded path of Divine aids we have learned many things.

8

Entheogens are a very powerful Magical & Spiritual tool, and their rules, as the rules of Yoga, must be obeyed to the letter. They are certainly not for all, but should not be denied to those who choose to use them to explore their own Divinity within. These rules include fasting before you trip, (whether a few hours or 24), and the vital importance of proper dosage and proper set & setting for the voyager. It was the good Dr. Timothy Leary who so graciously provided us with our early lysergic guidelines & Psychedelic Prayers. And from this, the latter day Psychedelic Culture moved forward.

So with the presence of Psychedelics, the modern Spiritual quest was given an entirely new & ancient tool for evolution.* Personal & collective. Those students of Yoga who, like their predecessors 2500 years before them (as related by Patanjali in the Yogic Sutras... Kaivalya Pada 1.) used Sacred herbs to further their yogic endeavors, found that the Yogic quest was facilitated by the discriminate use of these substances for focusing concentration and for ease in the awakening & moving of the Kundalini Energy, or the Soul. But double caution is given again; one should not mix psychedelics & Yogic endeavors unless they have fully physically, Spiritually, and mentally prepared themselves, and have total knowledge & ardent mastery of the complete procedure of Soul-release. *Otherwise you could cause severe disturbance to your mind, body, & life*. Rules must be followed if Destinations are to be reached. God would have it no other way.

9

For complete information on the yogic method, see my book-   Kundalini Yoga,
Beyond The Cosmic Mirage-
A Manual For Self-Liberation.

* "In the Mazatec and Zapotec regions of the mountains of Southern Mexico, the thaumaturges and *curanderos* continue, as they have for millennia, to employ an hallucinogenic potion in their magico-religious curing ceremonies. This potion is prepared from the seeds of certain species of morning glories, Turbina corymbosa and Ipomoea violacea. In the chemical-pharmaceutical research laboratories of Sandoz Ltd. in Basel, Switzerland, we have investigated the active principals of this drug, known as the ololiuhqui potion. These proved to be alkaloids found in ergot, namely lysergic acid amide and lysergic acid hydroxyethylamide, near relatives of lysergic acid diethylamide, the chemical name for LSD, also a product of ergot." *The Message of the Eleusinian Mysteries* by Albert Hoffman, appearing in Entheogens and the Future of Religion 1997.

Likewise in his book The Road to Eleusis, Albert Hoffman explains how it was most likely a LSD ergot fungus on the barley grains used in making the Sacred potion the *kykeon,* (which was administered to all of the initiates of the Greek Mystery Rites for almost 2,000 yrs. from 1500 B.C. to the fourth century A.D.), which was responsible for their revelations and precise understanding of the ecstatic state which is the nature of the next world & the state beyond death- "Elysium..."
Mystic (*Mystes*)- A candidate for the Elusian Mysteries.
10

By the end of the 20th century the use of chemical tools for mind expansion had reached a fine art. By knowing what substances to stay away from- heroin, cocaine, speed, downers, PCP, psychiatric pills... (which like many of these listed, can screw up your life, make you a zombie, & allow Evil to control your actions); nicotine, caffeine, alcohol*, white sugar, dead meat, pesticides, chemical food additives, mercury, fluoride, chlorine, aspartame, radiation, & TV; and what few to discriminately use- (cannabis, LSD, peyote, mescaline, psilocybin, ayahuasca perhaps, & on rare occasion maybe pharmaceutical MDMA), the wise & vibratorily-righteous Spiritual seeker could follow the most stunningly inlaid paths to Enlightenment; following the arcane signs and psychic footsteps left behind by all of God's Secret Agents before them.

Again I would point out and stress that the Yogic path may be dutifully followed with no entheogenic use at all, but absolute practice and purity of life & diet is a must. Self-purification is a natural prerequisite to becoming God.** It can be no other way.

Employing entheogens to aid in the awakening & moving of one's Kundalini should only be employed by advanced students of yoga and veteran trippers.

Likewise the use of entheogenic drugs for Spiritual advancement is meaningless unless an entire life change is pursued and the mind & body cleansed. The Yogic principals and practices provide the base of support necessary for the total transformation of the being into a candidate suitable for eternal citizenship in the next world.

11

*(This is not to eschew the relaxation properties of moderate alcohol use on occasion.)

** (The best high is perfect health. Unless you rid the body of the stored poisons within the system & stop further toxins from coming in, you're only circulating more and more toxins throughout the body- leading to fatigue, stagnation, & disease. If you want to feel really superb, it works to detoxify, eat whole pure foods, and tune into the Divine through yoga & meditation.)

PLUS FOUR,n. (++++) "A rare and precious transcendental state, which has been called a 'peak experience,' 'religious experience,' 'divine transformation,' a 'state of Samadhi,' and many other names in other cultures. It is not connected to the +1, +2 and +3 of the measuring of a drug's intensity. It is a state of bliss, a *participation mystique,* a connectedness with both the interior and exterior universes, which has come about after the ingestion of a psychedelic drug, but is not necessarily repeatable with a subsequent ingestion of that same drug. *If a drug (or technique or process) were to be discovered which would consistently produce a plus four experience in all human beings, it is conceivable that it would signal the ultimate evolution, and perhaps the end of, the human experiment.*" **TIHKAL** Alexander & Ann Shulgin pg. 607

Entheogen *n.* (*lit.* generate god or spirit within)
1. psychoactive sacrament; a plant or chemical substance taken to occasion spiritual or mystical experience. *Example:* peyote cactus used in the Native American Church. 2. hallucinogen; psychedelic.
(From Entheogens and the Future of Religion
The Council on Spiritual Practices 1997.)

13

CHAPTER 3

After Kundalini Yoga, meditation, & LSD, the next major tool for the highly inquiring mind in the Evolution of Enlightenment was the use of entheogenic tryptamines.

A tryptamine is "a naturally occurring compound found in both the animal and plant kingdoms. It is an endogenous component of the human brain."
THIKAL A. & A. Shulgin pg.∇

Within the plant kingdom lies the Kingdom of God. Plants were here before people and hold a great storehouse of Spiritual knowledge & healing powers. Healing plants for the body and Enlightening plants for the mind. In the Old World there were 15 known plant hallucinogens; in the New World over 100. These drugs are not of a narcotic nature, but are rather of a mind expansive nature dealing with the world of The Spirit.

There are two branches of the plant kingdom in which psychedelics are found- the flowering fungi & the flowering plants. Within these it has been discovered that it is the plant's alkaloids, or nitrogen containing compounds, which cause hallucinations.

In plants there are 4 main psychoactive alkaloid derivations:

Tropane- Datura (Jimsonweed, Devilweed) Evil. <u>**Never**</u>
<u>**Do**</u>.

Isoxazole- Mushrooms

Phenylethylamine- Peyote (From which Mescaline is
derived.)

Indole- LSD, DMT, 5-MEO-DMT, Bufotinene, Ibogane,
Harmine.

14

The Indoles are made up of a nucleus of tryptamine, derived from the amino acid tryptophan, which is also present in our diet. Tryptamines then, are Indole Alkaloids. Seratonin, a main mood-changing chemical neuro-transmitter, is also an Indole Alkaloid. It is the alkaloid's interaction with the human brain which produce profound changes in consciousness. *Thus the short acting tryptamines are very closely related to the neuro-transmitters, if they're not actually neuro-transmitters. themselves.*

The human brain is a highly specialized & infinitely intricate creation of God. It runs the complex mechanisms through which we perceive and function in this world, and by which we may transcend to the next. The brain and indeed the consciousness process itself, is chemical (electrical & pure energy) in nature, and functions through the production and consumption of chemicals within the body & brain. These chemicals are imperative in the task of processing information by the brain and sending out instructions to the body. There are hundreds of such neuro-transmitters which help run the body and which are essential to physical life and comprehension.

The Pituitary & Pineal Glands play major roles in the production and secretion of chemicals which regulate and potentate vital bodily functions. The Pineal Gland produces many neuro-transmitters such as Seratonin & Melatonin, which are refined from amino acids in the diet and control important areas such as mood, sleep, and reproduction. Both the Pituitary & the Pineal Glands play key roles in the Yogic process of Samadhi. It is known that the Pineal may be regulated in its activity by meditative practice, and it is the Pituitary which performs this process.

Yoga is the mastery of bodily and mental processes, (breathing, body locks, concentration, visualization, & willpower),used to produce complete and ineffably profound transcendental changes in consciousness.

In the Yogic process, it is a tryptamine-based chemical carrier in the cerebro-spinal fluid in the spinal column* which, along with the pressure from the applied yogic hydraulic body locks, raises the awakened Soul up through the central canal of the spine and into the Third Eye. Once the Kundalini enters the Pituitary Gland, (*Third Eye*), a greater amount of this higher consciousness chemical is secreted, sufficient to propel the Soul across the top of the head (called the *Rainbow Bridge*), through the Pineal Gland, & out of the body.

So basically, my personal research (and hopefully others to follow) would indicate that the Yogic process floods the brain with a natural tryptamine (5-MEO-DMT) produced in the body itself, which triggers Cosmic Consciousness. Likewise it has been discovered that smoking 6-10 mg. of pure 5-MEO-DMT in a glass vapor pipe accomplishes the same thing. It dissolves the bounds between you & God. It unlocks The Door to Eternity with its proper chemical key. That which God made for the process.

*(Personal research leads me to conclude that this is most certainly 5-MEO-DMT; although other tryptamines, DET & DPT, have been shown to aid in the release of the Soul as well. It is Tryptamine based for sure.)

17

CHAPTER 4

Tryptamine-based indigenous religious compounds have traditionally dominated South American psychotropic cultures, with their knowledge in the North Americas being scant if not non-extant. They were used in those cultures in the form of snuff & brews, which literally "blew their mind" into the next world.

Although some folks & luminaries of the 60's had access to tryptamine experiences from underground labs, news of their use was brought to most lay persons' minds the same way the entire 60's was laid at their door- by the Beats. In the 50's. In fact, by the Godfather of the Beat himself- William S. Burroughs, our humble reporter. Burroughs was the 1st head we'd heard of who'd pursued the entheogenic tryptamines of South America; both finding them, trying them, & reporting back. Much of the lush hallucinatory imagery that's found in Naked Lunch came from Burrough's 1954 Columbian Yage experiences later described in The Yage Letters; letters written between himself and Allen Ginsberg. Ginsberg had followed Burrough's tracks to South America in 1960, and had several yage sessions himself.

Likewise in the 1950's, the main psychoactive ingredients of these South American snuffs were revealed to be the tryptamines DMT and 5-MEO-DMT-Dimethyltryptamine & Dimethyl-5-methoxytryptamine. Traditionally, the religious use of these entheogenic tryptamines was most pervasive in the N.W. Amazon and Upper Orinco area of South America: Peru, Brazil, Venezuela, Columbia, & Ecuador. Here you have a vast expanse of indigenous people living very close to the

Earth and having total commune with God. Whether it was Sacred snuffs such as Cohoba, or the brews and barks used for Divine Communion such as Yopo, Yage, Ayahuasca, or Virola Banisteriopsis, it was the tryptamines DMT & 5-MEO-DMT which constituted the main psycho-active compounds of these journey agents. Let's then, look at the DMT's...

The entheogenic compounds of DMT & 5-MEO-DMT, Dimethyltryptamine & Dimethyl-5-methoxytryptamine, are both naturally occurring tryptamine-based psychedelic agents which, apart from being found in the plant kingdom & other mammals, are found in and produced by the human body. DMT is a natural constituent of human blood and urine, and both DMT & 5-MEO-DMT are present in trace amounts in the human brain and cerebro-spinal fluid.

Many researchers believe that DMT & 5-MEO-DMT are also neuro-transmitters. (*Human brain studies-* 1970 Dr. Wolfgang Vogel Jefferson Medical College of Phila.) (*Cerebro-spinal fluid & brain studies-* 1975 Dr. Samuel Christian Univ. of Alabama, Bingham, Al.)

The DMT derivatives may be accumulated whole through the diet or made in the Pineal Gland from dietary components. The amino acid L-tryptophan is generally considered to be the basic structural component for production of the indolealkalylamines from the diet.

DMT was first synthesized in 1931 by the Englishman Richard Manske.

In 1957 Stephen Sazara at the National Institute of Drug Abuse first experimented with pure DMT taken intramuscularly.

5-MEO-DMT was isolated in 1954 by Stromberg from the seeds of the A. peregrina- (Yopo tree).

5-MEO-DMT was first tested by Alexander Shulgin, with Entheogenic effects reported with smoking 6-10 mg. free base.

20

In 1990, Dr. Rick Strassman at the University of New Mexico's School of Medicine in Albuquerque tested 60 subjects with DMT over a period of 5 years ultimately in search of the biological basis of the Spiritual Experience. His research is recounted in his seminal book, DMT The Spirit Molecule.

In 1964 after personal investigation, Timothy Leary referred to DMT as "This wondrous alkaloid," and discussed its "potential for production of the Religious Experience." Leary makes mention of it both in the *Psychedelic Review*, (issues #1, #7, & #8), and in The High Priest. Other reports are just as profound.

DMT The 15 Minute Trip Bigwood & Ott 1977
"It is unfortunate that such a unique & desirable drug as DMT is not freely available & widely used. We feel that anyone who likes entheogenic drugs would do well to try DMT if given the chance. Not only are the effects enjoyable, but most users are astonished to learn that a drug can so rapidly produce such profound effects which have such short duration. DMT may well be the quintessential "Wonder Drug," for the initiate cannot help but wonder at its awe-inspiring potency."

Legal Highs Adam Gottlieb 1973
"**5-MEO-DMT** Effects: Overwhelming psychedelic effects occur almost instantly, softening to a pleasant LSD-like sensation after 2-3 minutes. Total experience lasts 20-30 minutes. Some persons experience dizziness, disorientation, & sensations of pressure during the first

21

2-3 minutes, especially with larger doses. If this occurs it is best to relax & flow with the experience, because it will quickly pass and give way to more comfortable feelings. *One should not take 5-MEO-DMT on a full stomach, as pressure & nausea may occur.* The drug leaves no hangover or undesirable aftereffects. One usually feels pleasantly stimulated for several hours afterward. It may interfere with sleep if taken near bedtime. Because of intense initial effects **one should never use this substance driving.**

Very large doses, sufficient to cause heavy blood rush to the head, may rupture weak capillary in the brain. Continued to excess this might eventually impair mental functions.
(**Ed. note**- That would be a really <u>stupid</u> thing to do. Proper dosage, 6-10 mg. infrequently smoked will not do this.)   **MAO inhibitor.**"

Pharmacotheon: Entheogenic Drugs, Their Plant Sources & History. Jonathan Ott 1992
"As is the case with any entheogenic substance & particularly with the short-acting tryptamines which rocket the user immediately from everyday consciousness to the peak entheogenic state, set & setting is of crucial importance. DMT should never be used casually as a sort of marijuana." pg. 190
"After inhalation of a full dose of DMT in a single breath, the effects will be experienced in 10-15 seconds, usually before exhalation of the smoke. The peak effect occurs in less than 60 seconds, taking 2-3 minutes, during which most users are stunned & speechless."
pg. 191

"5-MEO-DMT- Dimethyl-5-Methoxytryptamine. Entheogenic at 5-10mg. smoked." pg. 434

"5-MEO-DMT; Like DMT, this drug is evidently not active orally. When smoked, it is about four times the potency of DMT. Shulgin conducted experiments with nine subjects, finding that smoking 6-10 mg. of the free base of 5-MEO-DMT produced an entheogenic effect starting in less than 60 seconds, reaching a peak in two to three minutes and lasting about 20 minutes (Shulgin in DeSmet 1983)." pg. 182

"**Peak Experience**- Archetypal experience of ego transcendence & unitive state of consciousness."
Psychedelics Encyclopedia Peter Stafford rev. 1993
Pg. 329

From Chocolate to Morphine: Everything You Need to Know About Mind Expanding Drugs. Weil/ Rosen 1993 rev. pg. 103
"A close chemical relative of DMT is 5-MEO-DMT. It gives an equally powerful rush when smoked, but instead of visual hallucinations, the smoker experiences a complete dissolution of reality."
Wow! (Is that mildly understated or what? In reality, the smoker experiences a complete dissolution of
The Illusion.)

TIHKAL- Tryptamines I Have Known & Loved

Alexander & Ann Shulgin 1997 pg. 553

With perhaps 20 mg. smoked- "This is a very strong hallucinogen. A 20 minute experience. The 5-MEO-DMT was much more relaxed (than the terrifying DMT), a kind of Cosmic Consciousness type of thing. I broke into a space similar to DMT but like receiving Grace."

25mg. 5-MEO-DMT smoked- "After 10 seconds or so inhaling the last of the smoke it began; with a fast rising excitement of wonder, & with an undertone of 'now you've done it', but dominated by a sense of 'Wow, this is It!' There was a tremendous sense of speed & acceleration. In perhaps 10 seconds these feelings built to an intensity I had never experienced before. The entire Universe imploded through my consciousness. It's as if the mind is capable of experiencing a very large number of objects, situations, & feelings, but normally perceives them one at a time. I felt that my mind was perceiving them all at once. There was no distance, no possibility of examining the experience. This was simply the most intense experience possible; a singularity, White Out." Wow again!

(**Ed. note**- Again, **this is way too large a dose for safety sake**. 6-10 mg. smoked is the area of optimal Spiritual access and will give one a just as mind-opening experience. *More than that may cause long-term psychological difficulties with re-integration into this world upon return.*)

24

Pharmacotheon Ott pg. 58-

"The essence of the experience conferred by entheogenic drugs is ecstasy, in the original sense of the much overused word- *Ek- Statis*, the withdrawal of the Soul from the body."
(Oxford dictionary compact edition pg. 83)

pg. 58, 59 -

"More specifically, it is an ineffable, spiritual state of grace, in which the Universe is experienced more as energy than as matter (Ott 1977); *a spiritual non-materialistic state of being* (Hoffman 1988). It is the heart & essence of shamanism; the archetypal religious experience. In the archaic world, and in the preliterate cultures which have survived in isolation into our time, shamanism and ecstasy represent the epitome of culture, the pinnacle of human achievement."

(Calvin 1991)

From these reports and others, it is obvious that the tryptamines have a supreme significance to the Spiritual seeker for accessing God. These substances have an ancient history of use for this purpose.

The religious use of DMT & DMT-related compounds, (5-MEO-DMT and Bufotenine, which comes from certain toads sweat glands), for commune with The Spirit World and for the transportation of the Soul to Heaven, far pre-dates the arrival of European colonists in the Western Hemisphere. In 1496, on Columbus' second trip to the New World, Ramon-Pane documented the use of an entheogenic snuff called *Cohoba* by the native peoples of Haiti. As we have seen, the main psychoactive ingredients of this snuff are DMT & 5-MEO-DMT. Thus the twilight dawn of "American history" begins with the documentation of now 500 years of undisputed use of entheogenic tryptamines for accessing The Godstate.

Actually Spiritual entheogenic practice stretches as far back as plants & minds intertwine,* and today is blossoming into a full blown religious revival with music, sacrament, dance, & trance. The rave scene, like the Grateful Dead phenomenon, is the natural evolution of the Entheogenic Spirit Source towards an expression of celebration and unity of being.

Thus it has taken the Western mind 500 years to open itself wide enough to traverse the same path to God which was regularly used (no problem, that's the way it's done...) by some of the first inhabitants of the "New World" that it came upon. Feeling a little Spiritually behind? This might be a good lifetime to catch up.

26

* **Pharmacotheon** Ott pg.168- "DMT, 5-MEO-DMT, & Bufotenine were all recently (Torres 1991) detected in two snuff samples from a 1200 yr. old burial site at San Pedro de Atacama in Northern Chile. The samples were found in bags attached to a mummy bundle, which also contained snuffing paraphernalia." (Also see page 46.)

It should also be noted that in 2019 in the journal Science Advances, it was reported that archeologists had unearthed a 2,500 year old gravesite in the Pamir Mountains in western China and had found 10 wooden bowls with THC residue in them; again illustrating the age-old use of this herb for ritual & medicinal purposes.

CHAPTER 5

With 5-MEO-DMT, the use of entheogens to assist in the Yogic process of achieving Spiritual Enlightenment, (*for enhanced concentration and added ease in the visualization, awakening, & moving of the Kundalini Energy*), was no longer necessary. For with 5-MEO-DMT smoked, it is the entheogen itself which transports the Soul to Heaven; whereas in the Yogic process, the 5-MEO-DMT is produced & secreted by the human body in sufficient quantity as to open the doorway to Heaven & propel the Soul Homeward.

So in effect, smoking 6-10 mg. of 5-MEO-DMT takes you to the same place that Yoga & all true forms of Enlightenment do- to the very Throne of God. In the presence of the Almighty. God is the only thing in the Universe... the Only Being there ever was or will be.

Everything that exists and everything you see in the material world is made of Godstuff- from pure vibrating energy. (The different forms in the material world are made from energy vibrating at different speeds.) Truly, The Grand Illusion. Cosmic in scope, yet only an iota of what God can do, make, & be; to be experienced by as many Souls or subjective minds that God has created to experience this world through, before they consciously evolve back to the Godstate Itself. So if God designed it this way and left a path behind, it could only be assumed that one should follow. One way or the other. For there is nothing like The Godstate- and we're all being kept from It by an intricate maze of evolutionary intent. One that only we can overcome ourselves. For the further down the path of Enlightenment you go, the closer to God you are, until you arrive There.

28

At the moment of Enlightenment, as the Soul merges with the Infinite, then you will understand It All. You will be filled with Holy Light and go Beyond. You will then find yourself amazingly immersed in *the electric vibrating vortex of ecstatic Love that is God.* You are an initiate into the Ancient Mysteries of Antiquity and this is your initiation. Whether you experience It through Kundalini Yoga, or whatever form has been further evolved by God for us to use.

At this time it is 5-MEO-DMT, (6-10 mg. smoked inside a glass vapor pipe), which is at the pinnacle of the Evolution of Enlightenment. It is the safest & most simple way to access God to date. God's most advanced delivery system yet. (DET & DPT may even be better!)

I have personally experienced the release of Kundalini through Yogic means several times and likewise the release of the Divine Energy through the Sacred voyage of 5-MEO-DMT, and they are essentially one & the same.* The approach is somewhat different, but the Flight Controller, landing, & Home terminal are the same. Terminally Divine. Those who go know.

* The main difference between achieving the Transcendental State through Yoga & achieving it through 5-MEO-DMT, is that *if you attain this bliss through Yoga, then all of your past karma is washed clean in reward for your efforts.* With 5-MEO-DMT, it is the experience itself and the knowledge bestowed through the experience which is the reward. One can work intently on karmic resolution and yogic endeavors from there.

29

Also, there is no danger of physical or neurological damage from the release of the Kundalni Energy if the spine hasn't been adequately stretched out, as in Yoga. This is because the smoked 5-MEO-DMT activates the Soul immediately; propelling It into the Third Eye instantly and then exiting the body through the Pineal Gland & out of the head in a flash. The yogic task of raising the Soul up the spine and piercing the spinal blockages is therefore not a concern.

NOTE- The intensity of the experience could be very negative for an unstable mind.

THIS THEN IS THE PROCESS:

5-MEO-DMT SMOKING TECHNIQUE
WARNING- MAO INHIBITOR- see pages 56-58
Fast from solid foods 3- 6-12- 24 hrs.
Do on a floor, couch, bed, space with lots of
comfortable pillows or padding.
Do in a space of privacy, away from others where
loud sounds won't bother anyone.
Have phone turned down & ringer off.
Music if used should be Spiritual/ soft/ spacey.
Dress should be comfortable with minimal
pressure on stomach area.
Do sitting in a reclined position or with room to
recline immediately after inhalation.
Have someone assisting to hold the pipe while you
draw, or to take the pipe from your hands
immediately after inhalation. Don't do alone.
**The psychological state of the individual is
extremely important. (For stable minds only.)
If one is anxious, tired, tense, unstable, etc.
5-MEO-DMT should not be taken. Likewise
release through Yogic means should not be
attempted.**
*This is an extremely intense experience, one of
ego-loss & Transcendence; tossed into a whirling
vortex of pure electrical light somewhere far
beyond the material world. It's Heavy.*
The Peak Experience.
It's a completely mind-blowing experience,
so expect your mind to be blown. Fear not.
It's the Godstate.
One usually feels excellent after the experience.
Time of travel- 0-10 sec. Length of stay- 20-30 min.
Visiting- *God*

31

Place **6-10mg**. **(6-10 mg. = .006-.010 grams)** of pure 5-MEO-DMT inside a glass vapor pipe and slowly heat from below, slowly melting the powder into smoke. Do not hold the flame too close to the bottom of the pipe or the powder will vaporize too rapidly to produce the amount of smoke required. If you hold it too close it can also taste extremely bad- like burning plastic. When the bubble chamber of the pipe is densely filled with smoke and the powder ceases to vaporize, then ingest as much of the smoke as you can, & hold it in tightly for 20-30 seconds. If need be, take another hit from the same bowl if there's still smoke in it, but do it quickly; for once the initial hit of 5-MEO-DMT enters your body you only have about 60 seconds to ingest more... after that the action of further inhalations is blocked from being effective. *Thus you must inhale a sufficient amount in the first minute to surpass the threshold & get you There.* When the effects hit immediately after inhalation, you will be stunned, fall back upon the pillows, & you'll be totally oblivious to this world. Have someone there to take the pipe from your hands, as you leave this world & melt into
The Divine.

Sometimes the subject will make strange sounds, loud moans, or strange movements (Kriyas) during the experience. All of this is normal. When the Soul is awoken through Yogic means the subject often writhes around or flops on the ground like a fish out of water, as the Kundalini travels up the spine, pierces the 3 body blocks, and passes into and out of the head. This is often accompanied by audio effects... the sound of high-pitched winds or interstellar space sounds. All of this is normal. That is why the Kundalini (yoga) phenomenon has always remained far from public scrutiny. It appears as a very strange proceeding, far too strange perhaps to be readily accepted or understood by the lay mind. Undoubtedly in times past many revelers in the Divine were put to death or burned at the stake, because this experience appeared as "possession by spirits" to those closed minds who were uninformed about God & reaching the Godstate.

"5MEO increases pulse rate and blood pressure, more so than DMT, but not to the extent of a whiff of amyl nitrate. 5MEO can also produce breathing irregularities which may take some getting used to. If one does not get a good dose of 5MEO all they will feel are some bodily symptoms and a slight alteration of consciousness, especially in the visual field."

The Essential Psychedelic Guide D.M.Turner pg. 54

(Ed. note- "breathing irregularities to get used to" does not mean the complete cessation of breath or turning blue and not breathing. One may need to softly remind the subject to continue breathing slowly & deeply. Smelling salts may be good to have on hand.

33

Beyond that, **I would wisely advise that one of the attendants of a 5-MEO-DMT session be proficient in mouth to mouth resuscitation in the very off chance of respiratory cessation & the necessity for assistance.** Proper dosage should forego any of this, but caution is always best. This is a Sacred experience, but one that must be properly prepared for.**)**

Proper dosage is extremely imperative. There is no need to take more than **6-10mg.** of 5-MEO-DMT, that will get you to God. Where else could you want to go? Any more will only make you miss your mark & perhaps go somewhere you probably don't want to be, and maybe won't come back from for quite awhile.
It only takes a tiny bit, and way too much doesn't look like very much. You must be <u>exact</u> in your calibrations.

For example: "With an unknown but **large** amount smoked- I observed the subject pass very quickly into an almost coma-like state. Within seconds his face became purple and his breathing stopped. I pounded his chest, and breathed for him, and he seemed to emerge in consciousness with the comment, 'This is absolute ecstasy.' He stopped breathing a second time, and a heart massage and mouth-to-mouth resuscitation was provided. Again, he recovered and managed to maintain a continuing consciousness and achieve a partial recovery. In the awake condition he was increasingly lucid, but on closing his eyes he became possessed with what he called 'The energy of terror.'

He could not sleep, as upon closing his eyes he felt threatened in a way he could not tolerate. Three days later, medical intervention with anti-psychotic medication was provided, which allowed the recovery of an acceptable behavior pattern in a few more days."

THIKAL Alexander & Ann Shulgin pg. 534

As with all psychedelics, proper dosage, proper outlook, and proper set & setting are vital to a safe, healthy, and positive experience. With these drugs a very little is a lot, and **exact dosage is required**. The proper dosage for 5-MEO-DMT is as small as 2 paper match-heads. **A precise digital/electron scale should be used to calculate the 6-10 mg. dosage. (A scale accurate to .001 grams. 6-10 mg. = .006-.010 grams.) Never do more.**

"DMT and related compounds may not be the proper psychedelics for those with high blood pressure."
     Psychedelics Encyclopedia Peter Stafford pg. 323

Warning-   5-MEO-DMT is a MAO Inhibitor. This means that there are certain foods & drugs that must be avoided for at least 24 hrs. before you tryp. These substances could potentially cause life-threatening complications (rise or drop in blood pressure, cessation of breath) if used concurrently. Although I've read some who say this is not really a concern with 5-MEO-DMT, I would strictly adhere to the list of things to be abstained from on pages 57 & 58 to avoid possible contradictions. Especially anti-histamines, Ephedrine, (which you shouldn't do anyway unless medically necessary), and all "energy drinks".

As Divinely deduced, to seek & attain Enlightenment is the Supreme Earthly Endeavor, but not the final step. That is a process of purity and of conscious intentional evolution on our part, so that we may indeed be acceptable for citizenship in the Higher World when our Earthly life expires. The ultimate lesson is Universal Compassion & Love, and existing in that space. This translates into adopting a lifestyle best resonant with the God-vibration. Prayer, meditation, a diet free of poisons, a mind free of the same, & good intent. Yoga transforms your human body into a form which opens up the life-flow from within and Above; more & more in a purifying evolutionary manner meant to build your vibratory Soul-vehicle for eternal existence in Heaven. That's why diet, stretching, breathing, & meditation are so important. That's God's honing process for Heaven... the way it was made by our Creator.

In this way you'll have made some headway by showing God that you have the discipline to clean up your act to the God-level. That you have the smarts to un-weave yourself from this tangled web of illusion and plot your own course Home. You can't do that with smack, or coke, or speed, or alcohol, or anti-depressants, or caffeine, or nicotine, or sugar, or TV, or pollution, or violence hounding your Soul. Wrong vibration.

If this wasn't a test it wouldn't matter, but it is and it does. To ignore that fact is only self-defeating; to acknowledge that is to work towards Eternal liberation and orgasmic form. Which in all honesty takes a lot of work, but not that much all things considered.

37

That, compared to countless lifetimes trapped in an ever rapidly deteriorating Earth-plane scenario... the choice is clear.

Move beyond the dinosaurs.

The Evolution of Enlightenment is to return yours and all Souls back to the eternal unity of God's Heavenly Body in as few a number of lifetimes as is humanly possible. It's the biggest revelation, purpose, mystery, adventure, liberation, joy, opportunity, & challenge that you've ever been given, so you better get going. For truly- "There's no place like Home."
OM SHANTI.

CHAPTER 6

The Psychedelic Culture has had a long and elegant history. With its mind revealing/world-transcending wonders, its history has been largely one of individual enlightenment & liberation, yet at the same time largely dominated by persecution throughout the ages.

From the persecution of the early Roman church, to the Inquisition, to the current U.S. government's War on Drugs. With its Saints & emissaries through the ages often driven Underground. Offering with Yoga, the tried and true Union with God, Enlightenment, Evolution, consciousness expansion, the overcoming of karma, & Eternal Liberation...

This is what we're looking for, is it not?

From the very Dawn of Enlightenment, through all the partakers of the Divine up until now: passing in our time from The Beats, through the 60's, through the illuminated halls of the Grateful Dead, and now filling the minds of those who share in ceremonial medicine gatherings and individual seekers of the mystical; psychoactive substances have always been here to show us The Way. It was psychedelics which gave rise to some of the earliest religious traditions. Entheogens are most likely the origin of religion itself. The Original Religion of ecstatic union with God. It is only their knowledge & access to which we've been denied at times, which has served to delay our collective Spiritual maturation.

5-MEO-DMT was made illegal as a Schedule I drug in 2011, and this is clearly a case of the un-Constitutional interference with our guaranteed Religious Freedoms.

Also it's a naturally made component of our physical body. Rationalize that.

40

There is no real potential for abuse of 5-MEO-DMT. It has no addictive qualities. As supremely pleasant as Heaven is, to get there on a regular basis, Yoga is the key. The intensity of the 5-MEO-DMT experience personally precludes the desire for immediate repetition, and Its lessons last a lifetime. The lessons learned apply to this world & our evolution from here to There. It certainly wouldn't be necessary to do the 5-MEO-DMT experience more than once every many years or even once in a lifetime for that matter. For it shows you where you could reside if you wisely spend the rest of your life in expectant preparation. The key is not to just go there again, but to evolve yourself here on Earth so that you may reside There forever. The glimpse is no substitute for The Existence.

5-MEO-DMT is by no means a "recreational drug". It is a Sacrament. It is a direct conduit to God, and if any lawmaker or governing body disagrees, then simply let them try 6-10mg. 5-MEO-DMT in the safe and prescribed manner, and they will see for themselves. Undoubtedly most would shrink back from this opportunity, afraid of the unknown and certainly of God. Their argument holds no validity then; for the beneficialness & blessedness of this substance can be proven with use, and at the very same time, cannot be disproven by non-use. Abuse could only come through ignorance or irresponsible use. Ignorance is cured through truthful knowledge, and irresponsible use has its own non-rewards; which is the result of using anything in the wrong way. That's one of the lessons we are on Earth to learn. Aspirin, cars, hammers, gasoline, firearms, money, a kiss, trust, political power; all of these have a potential for abuse if misused. Yet none of these will get you to God if properly used. The religious use of 5-MEO-DMT completely outweighs the minuscule-non-existent potential for its abuse. Fact.

Entheogens* offer the most immediate and direct form of communication with God that we've got, and should not be discriminated against because of ignorance and fear. Instead, if so chosen, they should be responsibly & religiously used in the privacy of one's own mind for the highest purpose on Earth-

the Evolution of Enlightenment.

For only you are responsible for your Soul, and to hang out among Earth-binding entrapments will only get you where you are now- back on the Earth plane trying to figure it all out. Go beyond all of that, and there'll be no question as to the wisdom of your direction once you've reached Home. We are primarily Spiritual Beings. The Supreme purpose of this Earthly trip is to reclaim our Godhead. To go beyond form once and for all. This opportunity should not be denied any informed, prepared, and responsible adult by anyone.

Entheogens should be treated by all as the Sacred gifts from God which they are. They are a major part of the Divine Plan. They are not for all. Or perhaps, all are not for them. No matter- Yoga, prayer, & meditation will get you There, and indeed, these should be your first steps towards God.

* (As well as prayer, meditation, & Yoga .
Remember, **Yoga alone will get you There.**)

"...The Old Wisdom does have something to give the world of tomorrow, and that priceless gift is the knowledge of entheogenic plants & their use. Encoded in the genes of entheogenic plants are instructions for the bio-synthesis of molecules which open us up to the wonder & mystery inherent in the Universe & in ourselves; ancient wisdom... residing in every human heart & Soul, awaiting a chemical or other key for its unfurling."

Pharmacotheon Jonathan Ott pg. 242

"The destruction of the sanctuary at Eleusis at the end of the 4th century of our era marked the final downfall of the ancient world in Europe, & for the next millennium the Theocratic Catholic Church vigorously persecuted every vestige of ecstatic religion which survived, including revival movements. By the time of the "discovery" of the New World, Europe had been beaten into submission, the witches & heretics mostly burned, & ecstasy was virtually expunged from the memory of the survivors. For the Catholics & Protestants after them, to experience ecstasy, to have religious experiences was the most heinous heresy, justifying torture & being buried alive. Is it any wonder that today we have no place for Ecstasy?

In the New World, however, the Age of Entheogens & ecstasy lived on, and although in 1620 The Inquisition in Mexico formally declared the use of entheogenic plants like Peyotl to be a heresy and the Church vigorously extirpated this use and tortured & executed Indian Shamans, ecstasy survives there even now.

44

It bears witness to the integrity of the New World Indians that they braved torture & death to continue with their ecstatic religion- they must have been bitterly disappointed in the 'placebo sacrament' of the Christian Eucharist, which is a placebo entheogen; and it is largely as a result of the modern cult of Tenonacatl discovered by R. Gordon Wasson in 1955, that the modern use of entheogens began. Even though myriad justifications for the modern laws against entheogens have been offered up, the problem modern societies have with these drugs is fundamentally the same problem the Inquisition had with them, the same problem the early Christians had with the Eleusinan Mysteries- religious rivalry. Since these drugs tend to open peoples eyes & hearts to an experience of the Holiness of the Universe."

Pharmacotheon Jonathan Ott pg. 59

"The Divine *infuses* the entheogenic plant & its user."

Ott

"Virtually all of the entheogens, or their natural prototypes, have already proven their worth in induction of ecstatic states in shamanism (Halifax 1979; Halifax 1982; La Barre 1970; La Barre 1972; La Barre 1979; La Barre 1980; Rosenbohm 1991; Wasson 1961); and in the catalyst of 'religious experiences' (Clark 1969; W.H. Clark 1970; Felice 1936; Heard 1963; Leary 1964; Leary & Alpert 1963; Leary *et al* 1964; Masters & Houston 1966; Metzner 1968; Paz 1967; Ricks 1963; Watts 1962; Watts 1963; Zaehner 1957; Zaehner 1972; Zinberg 1977).

45

Well-known examples of shamanic use of entheogens, which will be documented thoroughly in this book, are: primordial Siberian shamanic use of the fly-agaric, *Amanita muscaria;* the Mexican shamanic use of *teonanacatl,* the psycilocibin mushrooms; pan-Amazonian shamanic use of ayahuasca in South America; use of tryptamine-containing snuffs in the Caribbean and Amazonia; divinatory use of ergoline alkaloid-containing morning glory seeds in Mexican shamanic healing, and North American shamanic use of the peyotl cactus.

The value of entheogens to organized religions has been amply demonstrated by the 2,000 year survival of the famous Eleusinian Mystery religion of the ancient world (an annual mass initiation employing an entheogenic potion containing ergoline alkaloids); Wasson *et al* 1978; and the modern examples of the 'Native American Church' and 'The Peyote Way Church of God' employing *peyotl* as a sacrament (La Barre1938; La Barre 1970; Mount 1987; Stewart 1987) and South American Christian Churches incorporating *Daime (ayahuasca)* as a sacrament (Henman 1986; Liwszyc et al 1992; Lowy 1987; MacRae 1992; Prance 1970). Perhaps using these historical and modern examples as models will aid us in designing institutions to foster religious experiences in human users (Hoffman 1989). There is a place in the modern world both for organized entheogen-based religions and the shamanic model of small-scale cultic or individual use; for group communion for solitary psychonautic 'travels in the universe of the soul' (Gelpke 1981)- not to mention for medicinal use." **Pharmacotheon** Jonathan Ott pg. 69

46

CHAPTER 7

Although DMT is also a primary ingredient in many of the South American psychotropic journey agents, I personally believe that it is 5-MEO-DMT which should be respectfully used for the chemical induction of The Religious Experience. This is because 5-MEO-DMT is a reliable vehicle for this experience; whereas DMT itself is so unpredictable that even if it could have the ability to take you to those spaces, there is no guarantee that it would, or would any % of the time, if ever. This fact was noted in Rick Strassman's DMT research. He was surprised at the few mystical-type experiences his subjects had on DMT, having fully expected that it would facilitate these to a far higher degree.

To quote D.M. Turner in **The Essential Psychedelic Guide** pg. 52-

"What one will experience on DMT is impossible to predict. It can range from heaven to hell, cyberspace to jeweled palaces, fear or personified evil, visions of jungle animals, contacts with extra-terrestrials, links with ancient spirits, or adventures with faeries or elves. The DMT user should be prepared for anything."

"Many users, including myself, have felt possessed by various spirits while on DMT, as if becoming a medium and channeling alien thoughts. This can be quite heavy. It has been generally positive for myself and the people I've smoked DMT with, but I've heard stories from others who have experienced the other extreme."

"In recent years DMT has become quite notorious in the psychedelic underground, primarily through the writings of Terrance McKenna. And despite the fact that it is rare and highly sought after, once it becomes available to those who are seeking it, very few people use it frequently after a short period of initial use. I've assumed that many people have joy rides for their first several trips, then have an experience which is extremely frightening or intense, leaving them intimidated about continuing DMT use. However, I like a friend's recent explanation for this observation better; 'DMT gets progressively *weirder* as you keep smoking it.' "

(Ed. note- <u>I would personally advise against doing DMT at all</u>. It makes you "dingy," eroding your brain and speech functioning over time.

Sometimes there can be a thin line between being adventurous & putting yourself through Hell...
"To boldly go where no one's returned from before.")

<u>I would likewise say the same about Ketamine.</u>
Ketamine is a general anesthetic which some people use to access higher spaces. Ketamine can get to be heavily psychologically addicting and be more of a side-track than path towards any sort of Enlightenment. Again, <u>if you are looking for the Truth & that which lies Beyond, 5-MEO-DMT is the chemical Key to Eternity, Yoga is the physical key</u>, (which unlocks the chemical key within the body). And if you're looking for jeweled palaces & everything else warmly psychedelic, try Mescaline. Mescaline (that is extracted from Peyote) is the very best. Those who enjoy Ecstasy would love Mescaline, and it's not toxic to the system. (<u>As X is.</u>)
It's the very best...

Again D. M. Turner-

"A psychedelic dose of Ketamine moves one towards a state of unconsciousness where a surgeon could operate on them. The normal reaction abilities that prevent us from accidents and death are suspended while on Ketamine."

"After taking Ketamine some 100 times I've noticed that it's fairly easy to miss the mark, and wind up with an experience that is nothing like what I've described above."

"A major concern regarding safe use of Ketamine is its very high potential for psychological addiction. A fairly large percentage of those who try Ketamine will consume it non-stop until their supply is exhausted. I've seen this in friends I've known many years who are regular psychedelic users and never before have had problems controlling their drug consumption. And I've seen the lives of several people who developed an addiction to Ketamine take downward turns. After about two years of once-per-week Ketamine use I even found that I had developed an addiction. Although it was less severe than what I've described above, it took considerable effort to break the cycle of repeatedly using it, even though I was aware of detrimental effects that it was causing. Since that time I've used Ketamine only occasionally, but find that I must continually exercise a high degree of will power to prevent myself from falling into a pattern of regular use. I've seen very few people who can use it in a balanced manner if they have access to it."

Ed. note- D. M. Turner died in the late 1990's while experimenting with (I was told) Ketamine in his bathtub. The bathtub was his preferred setting for doing Ketamine and other combinations of drugs. Safe as some may think it is, this may be reason enough to not get involved with the Big K.

Turner was one who experimented extensively with multiple combinations of substances, and his books are interesting reads, even if one were not inclined to mix their vehicles as he. I'm not personally into all that, as I've found that there's a lot of sidetracks in outer space, especially when you're dealing with Inner Space. Especially if transcending the Illusion's your goal. Thus I would say that the DMT & Ketamine experience are largely just part of the rest of the illusion, and not recommended to reach God. There are many pitfalls on the pathway to both Paradise & perdition, so choose your way with care. Many side-roads never return to The Way. Again, the Yogic road is the path to embark on. It's the most trusted, and is the only path needed to reach Home.

There are two other psychedelic chemicals that have been reported on in association with The Mystical Experience. They are DET (DIETHYLTRYPTAMINE) & DPT (DIPROPYL-TRYPTAMINE). These are both homologous tryptamine derivatives of DMT, whose effects are longer acting & more potent, yet more subtle than DMT. As I've had no experience with either of these agents, I really can't give you any information, except for what I've listed below from other sources. They may well be a better vehicle than 5-MEO-DMT. Only further research will tell...

DET

DET (Diethyltryptamine) was first tested in Hungary in 1957 (Szara) and again in 1959 (Boszormenyi). It differs from DMT in length of duration & intensity.

"A similar difference in time occurs for smoking the drugs. The effect of smoked free base of DMT commences virtually immediately and lasts only ten to fifteen minutes, whereas smoked DET free base requires a few minutes to be felt and lasts for about one to two hours. There are qualitative differences between the two compounds as well. While DMT has a dramatic sledgehammer-like power, the effect of DET is more subtle, and the drug is less likely to provoke anxiety and panic states which may occur following DMT administration. This fact, combined with the idyllic one to three hour duration of effect, makes DET one of the most desirable of all entheogenic agents, particularly advantageous for users naive to entheogens. As the Boszormenyi group commented: 'we believe DET to be

51

the best and least noxious psychotogenic agent known thus far, which seems to have an unquestionable therapeutic effect as well" (Boszormenyi 1959). DET is reportedly active orally at high doses (Shulgin 1976)."
Pharmacotheon Jonathan Ott pg. 180

"DET doesn't have the visual impact of DMT but does invoke intense, pleasurable states of mind, which last for about an hour when the substance is smoked. *Meditating users have noticed that they can lock themselves into a lotus position much more easier than before. The DET experience can be built upon by repeated inhalations, with some users reporting that they have begun to 'vibrate' and 'raise their Kundalini Energy'.*

Some users find that their eyes turn backward, as in a state of religious ecstasy. Among those who have experienced DET with religious intensity is Alan Birnbaum, from the Native American Church of New York: 'DET was the first psychedelic which convinced me that the psychedelic is a Primeval Light Being which is God, the Creator...' "
Psychedelics Encyclopedia Peter Stafford pg. 328

DET was listed as a Schedule I drug by the Controlled Substances Act of 1970. This of course, makes us all illegal all of the time; because of the DMT & DMT derivatives within our blood, urine, cerebro-spinal fluid, & brain.

DPT

DPT (Dipropyltryptamine) is another candidate for possible exploration.

"DPT was first tested by Szara in animals (Szara 1962), and later found to have properties similar to DET in human subjects (Faillace *et al* 1967; Szara 1970). *This intriguing compound has been explored as a means to induce "peak experiences" (mystical or religious experiences; see Maslow 1962) in terminal cancer patients; ...isolated from distractions by blindfolds and headphones playing classical music, peak experiences were indeed induced in some subjects* (Grof & Halifax 1977; Richards 1975; Richards *et al.* 1977).

Like DET, this compound is reportedly active orally in high doses (Shulgin 1976), and the free base is reportedly entheogenic when smoked (Stafford1983.)"

Pharmacotheon Jonathan Ott pgs. 180-181

"DPT has not been very widely used to date, but those who have tried it seem to agree that it does produce psychedelic or "peak" experiences." "Adam Birnbaum writes of DPT, *'some people have reported to be immediately immersed in the light on the first toke'.*"

"...the most intense part of a DPT experience is over in about 20 min."

"In the January-March 1977 *Journal of Psychedelic Drugs*, five doctors on the Spring Grove team (Spring Grove Hospital near Baltimore) discussed their findings about The Peak Experience Variable in DPT-Assisted Psychotherapy with Cancer Patients. They expressed their opinion that among the many altered states of psychedelic consciousness, peak experiences 'are probably among the most difficult to facilitate... but we now possess a technology that can evoke peak experiences with sufficient potency and reliability to permit us to study their impact on human behavior.'

They undertook to test such a possibility with DPT, administering it to thirty-four cancer patients who were expected to live at least three months and who were suffering major psychological stress. The goal was to evoke what William James called the "noetic" quality of peak experiences, about which he had written:

'...although so similar to these states of feeling, these mystical states seem to those who experience them to be also states of knowledge. They are states of insight into depths of truth unplumbed by the discursive intellect.'

Collected data indicated 'clinical improvement of greater magnitude for the group of peakers than for the group of non-peakers.' "

"In a comment also pertinent for anyone considering use of DPT, they observed that when a peak experience does occur, its continuing relevance for daily living may be strongly dependent on the degree to which the associated insights are assimilated or transferred into the everyday self-concept and world view of the patient.' "

Psychedelics Encyclopedia Peter Stafford pgs. 322-329

DPT is I believe, legally legal at this time, but subject to classification as illegal DMT analogues under the ubiquitous Controlled Substances Analogue Act of 1986.

"There is a rather remarkable religious group known as the Temple of the True Inner Light, in New York City, which has embraced as its Eucharist DPT, which they refer to as a powerful Angel of the Host. Their communion is confirmed by either the smoking or the drinking of the sacrament, and they have been totally unbothered by any agency of the Federal Government, as far as I know. It is not as if they were unknown. Quite on the contrary. I had on one occasion received a request for information on the drug from a reporter who was writing a story on DPT and its use in the church. I asked him just how he had gotten my name, and he told me that it was given to him by someone within the D.E.A. Someone, sometime, should write an essay on contemporary religions, as to why DPT has flown, why peyote forever struggles, and LSD and marijuana have bombed out, when tied to religion? Is there something about a faith being an "approved" religion? Who gives his approval? Who decides the applicability of the First Amendment, which explicitly states that 'Congress shall make no law respecting an establishment of religion, or prohibiting the free exercise thereof'? I wish the True Inner Light congregation Godspeed, if you will excuse the expression. My impression of them from my correspondence has left me totally convinced of their integrity and dedication."

THIKAL Alexander Shulgin pg. 430

MAO INHIBITORS

"MAO (monamine oxidase) is an enzyme produced in the body, which breaks down certain amines and render them harmless and ineffective. An MAO inhibitor interferes with the protective enzyme and leaves the body vulnerable to these amines. A common substance such as tyramine, which is usually metabolized with little or no pharmacological effect, may become dangerous in the presence of an MAO inhibitor and cause headache, stiff neck, cardiovascular difficulties, and even death. MOA inhibitors may intensify and prolong the effects of other drugs (CNS depressants, narcotic analgesics, anticholinergics, benzodiazepine antidepressants etc.) by interfering with their metabolism."

"Among the materials which may be dangerous in combination with MAO inhibitors are sedatives, tranquilizers, antihistamines, narcotics, and alcohol; any of which can cause hypotensive crisis (severe blood pressure drop); and amphetamines (even diet pills), mescaline, asarone, nutmeg (active doses), macromerine, ephedrine; oils of dill, parsley, or wild fennel; beer, wine, cocoa, aged cheeses and other tyrosine-containing foods (tyrosine is converted into tyramine by bacteria in the bowel)- any of which can cause hypotensive or hypertensive (severe blood pressure rise) crises."

"Most primitive people fast or at least abstain from certain substances for several days prior to taking a sacrament. Substances most universally avoided are alcohol, coffee, meat, fat, and salt."

Legal Highs Adam Gottlieb

"MAO (Mono-Amine-Oxidase) is an enzyme in the body which breaks down certain foods and chemicals. If one has these foods or chemicals in their system while taking an MAO inhibitor they will not be broken down, which can result in discomfort, illness, or even death. Following this section is a list of items not to be taken with MAO inhibitors. Prior to taking an MAO inhibitor I review this list and do a double check on what's in my system. I've also found it useful to memorize this list of items so I don't eat any foods that will make me ill while using MAO inhibitors.

The following psychedelics are MAO inhibitors; 5-MEO-DMT & the HARMALA ALKALOIDS. Many prescription anti-depressant drugs are also MAO inhibitors. They should not be taken in combination with the foods or drugs listed below.

Items not to be taken in combination with MAO inhibitors

VERY DANGEROUS

Sedatives & Tranquilizers   Macromerine
Tryptophan- large doses   Red Wine
Antihistamines
Tyrosine- large doses
Narcotics
Phenelalanine- large doses
Amphetamines (Ed note- also Ritalin, Adderall, Ecstasy)
Alcohol
Asarone/Calamus, Ephedrine   (**Ed**. Energy Drinks)
Aged Cheeses

POTENTIALLY DANGEROUS
Coffee
Beer, White Wine
Cocoa, Nutmeg- large doses
Yeast Extract   Oil of Dill- large doses
Pineapple, Oil of Parsley- large doses
Sauerkraut, Liver
Pickled Herring
Soy Sauce, Figs & raisins
Cream, Yogurt
Avocados (especially overripe)
Bananas (especially overripe)
Prescription or Over the Counter Medicines & Supplements
   Unless one is certain that these can be taken with MAO inhibitors they should discontinue use long enough for them to pass out of their system before taking the MAO inhibitor."
   THE ESSENTIAL PSYCHEDELIC GUIDE D.M. Turner.

PEYOTE PREPARATION

The process for cleaning Peyote is as follows. First off, you must remove the Strychnine from the Peyote buttons carefully & thoroughly to avoid becoming sick and vomiting. The Strychnine lies in the center of the button, in spots on the cacti exterior, and within the button as well. They are tufts of cottony fibers which pull out as clumps of individual white hairs. The Strychnine inside the buttons appears as round BB size husk-covered balls. The buttons must be cleaned with care. Break each one into small pieces, removing as you go, all of the silken fibers, while washing the pieces repeatedly in a strainer. When working with live buttons, the juice will be absorbed through your fingertips and you will be dosed unless you wear rubber gloves. If the buttons are dried, remove the fibers on top, outside, and the husk-covered round balls of Strychnine inside with an x-acto type razor knife very carefully, chipping each layer of the button away removing the solid looking white pieces of Strychnine on the top of the button and the round brown husk-covered fibers within. Wash the pieces repeatedly, taking up to half an hour to clean each button. Then mix the small pieces in honey, chewing slowly & thoroughly.

When harvesting live Peyote cacti, it's imperative that you only cut the top of the cactus above ground level to allow the plant to live and produce future buttons.

ENTHEOGENS

ENTHEOGENS

Entheogen *n*. (lit. Generate god or spirit within)
1. Psychoactive sacrament; a plant or chemical substance taken to occasion spiritual or mystical experience. *Example:* peyote cactus used in the Native American Church. 2. Hallucinogen; psychedelic.
(From Entheogens and the Future of Religion.
The Council on Spiritual Practices 1997.)

ENTHEOGENS & YOGA

Patanjali, author of the Yoga Sutras (the original yoga text at least 2-5,000 yrs. old) relates in the Sutras in Kalvalya Pada 1, about the yogins of the time using Sacred and medicinal herbs to further their Spiritual practice & yogic attainments.

In his book, Integral Yoga, The Yoga Sutras of Pantanjali, Swami Satchidananda comments on this sutra saying of Pantanjali- "He also gives us some clues about the people who get some experiences through their LSD & Marijuana. Your so-called "grass" is an herb, is it not? Mushrooms could be considered herbs also."

So too, the present day students of yoga have found that their yogic quest can be readily facilitated by the discriminate light use of Entheogenic Sacraments; for enhanced concentration and ease in the awakening & moving of the Kundalini Energy, or the Soul.

This is an extremely advanced technique, optional, and not at all necessary to the yogic process of Soul-release fore-described in this book. One should not attempt to mix entheogens and yogic endeavors unless

62

they have spent the pre-requisite 1- 2 years in direct preparation for the experience. That is, stretching the spine, daily practice for hours, and learning the yogic procedures for release inside out, to the point of intimate familiarity. Only then, with the proper psychedelic preparatory forays under their belt, should one attempt to combine the two; and only when actually attempting to awaken one's Soul.

Never do entheogens and aimlessly mess with your Sacred Energy- it's VERY DANGEROUS.

In Terence McKenna's fine book, Food of the Gods, he notes the direct connection between the dawn of human civilization, humankind's awakening Spiritual & intellectual consciousness, and the primal use of hallucinogenic mushrooms. Peyote, mescaline, and early ergot forms of LSD all had their influence as well.

It's these same Entheogenic substances which can aid in the yogic endeavor. *Aiding in the awakening & release of ones Kundalini Energy (Soul) is the truest & highest purpose of Psychedelics.*

Psilocybin mushrooms, LSD, Peyote, and Mescaline in **moderately low doses** will give the adept an edge on concentration, attention, procedure, and the visualized direction of both the prana flowing inward & through the etheric body, and the Kundalini as It stirs from Its slumber and rises into & up the spine. It's especially effective in this endeavor, as the adept already has their eyes, ears, and mind focused entirely inward; and it is

63

in this inner world that the acute awareness and exactitude of the process of Soul activation is necessary for success- especially in the area of breath control and employing the body locks and the intense pressure needed to squeeze the Kundalini up the spine. It is almost a super-human endeavor, and the Entheogens make the task much easier. Especially awakening the Kundalini and visually directing It where to go. Remember, only **moderately low doses** should be employed.

So the use of Entheogenic substances <u>are by no means required</u> for the ardent and rightly patient yoga practitioner. Their success is guaranteed by their journey. But likewise, tools are meant to be used by those who choose to do so. For when <u>properly used</u> tools, by definition, can make an arduous endeavor easier to accomplish.

THE ENTHEOGENIC EXPERIENCE

First of all, you should fast for at least 3-24 hrs. before you trip. A good meal and vitamins taken somewhat before that is a good idea, to give you the nourishment required for your journey. Tripping is an energetic experience, and can take a lot out of you. Food will inhibit the action of the Sacrament, making it harder to get off, and once tripping, may upset your stomach and disrupt the experience. Later however, you may want to replenish with fruit, food, or juices while hiking etc. Generally though, one has little or no appetite while taking Entheogens.

Secondly, you must choose with care where you trip and with whom, if anyone. It's best to trip with a trusted friend or friends and to dose lightly. Environment is 90% of the psychedelic experience, (set & setting), and tripping in nature and the woods always offers wondrous times. It's a good idea to have a sanctuary or secure place where you will not be disturbed by people and the normal going-ons of the world. Dealing with the "real world" can be done, but at times, can be a bit much or too much. If so, act natural.

Tripping rooms are especially nice, where one feels naturally comfortable surrounded by Spiritual decor, psychedelic art, oriental rugs, and Eastern & psychedelic music. These bring out the best in your head. The paintings of Peter Max, Maxfield Parrish, Daniel Merriam, Salvador Dali, & M.C. Escher are well suited for the Entheogenic experience. Incense is enticing.

Some Entheogenic journeys can be extremely visual in nature. Especially mescaline. Everything turns bejeweled in sparkling arabesque patterns. It's really quite stunning. Sunrises and sunsets are especially impressive. The hour or so after sunset, when the sky moves through its innumerable shades of blue and the stars magically appear one by one is my favorite. And of course, the best is the full-on night sky. The millions of stars. If you lay down and watch them for 20-30 minutes, they will start to melt and sway in the heavens; dancing through the night sky like a field of cosmic fireflies.

Hallucinations may be as subtle as a redwood table flowing like a miniature river, or the person you're talking to turning into a full-blown lion, while continuing on with the conversation. Those things are rare, but not unseen. Those type of things you should always view with a grain of salt. Go with the flow, as they say.

It should be duly noted that sometimes the perceptions one has while tripping may not be what's really going on. This tends to happen with high dosages, if so facto. Thus the practicality of having someone with you on your journey, and perhaps someone who is not under the influence.

Driving should technically be avoided, except in real necessity, for obvious reasons. Veteran Entheogenic users on low doses are the ones who, in those cases, should drive.

Animals are extremely nice to be around, as they are already hooked into the flow of the Universe. Dogs are the very best.

Preparation is important, making sure that you have everything you might need on your journey with you before you start. Water, warm clothes, coat, rain gear, food, flashlight, first-aid kit, ID, music, herb, etc. should be considered. Phones may be good in the off chance of an emergency, but definitely keep the ringer off or battery out if you value your privacy. Don't even look at the T.V. You shouldn't anyway...)

Music is one of the major environmental stimuli which lend to a positive tripping experience. The better the sound system, the better. The type of music is a matter of one's own preference, but there's a whole genre' of music called Acid Rock for a reason.

The "Psychedelic Sound" is just that. The music of the Beatles, Donovan, the Doors, Jefferson Airplane, the Grateful Dead, Hot Tuna, Jimi Hendrix, the church, and Pink Floyd will certainly give your mind a place to go. Eastern music and the ragas of Ravi Shankar are extremely engaging. So are Indian chants. Classical music is expansive... The excellent Beatles movie, *Yellow Submarine*, is certainly a good trip to take. Listening & dancing to live music is one of the finest things to do while Entheogenning.

Your first trips will most likely be highly introspective-sorting out the odds & ends of your existence and fitting them back into place. You'll be amazed by the intricacies of nature and God's creation. Meditation provides an unending space to traverse.

Entheogens can open one's deepest center of compassion; revealing and amplifying feelings of unity, oneness, love, and fellowship towards God, nature, humankind, and especially towards those sharing the experience. Two people tripping together can serve as a beautiful exploratory experience, establishing a magical bond of love and trust that can last far beyond a lifetime.

Tripping is essentially non-verbal, so while language has its place within the experience, silence should be welcome. Oftentimes your senses will function at a heightened state of awareness, and you become more attentive to that which is around you. This is especially true with the sense of touch, as you can feel the electromagnetic energy flowing through yourself and others. This in turn, can elevate the acts of massage and lovemaking to the realm of the Sacred & Spiritually erotic.

Tripmeister Terence McKenna's ubiquitous RX for the psychedelic voyager was-

5 grams dried mushrooms in total darkness,
which would certainly lend to a state of heightened sensory awareness.

(You could look into Terrance's left eye & go right into outer space...)

My personal preference used to be to trip almost exclusively alone, (except at shows), thus allowing the communion between the Entheogen & the mind to be complete, absorbing the knowledge offered by the experience and offered by God. Psychedelics are a communication link between the Higher Spiritual Powers & your mind, so tripping with others may be conducive to this process or not, depending upon who you're with.

68

If you do trip with others, it's best if they are stable and of a flowing nature; as it can be most frustrating to be tripping and caught up in other people's hang-ups. The Entheogenic experience bares your Soul and can place one's ego in an extremely vulnerable state, sensitive to real or imagined negativity or criticism. Thus treat others with warmth, respect, patience, and with a compassionate understanding of the state.

Near the end of a trip, when the effects of the psychedelics are waning, it is nice to take a hot shower or bath and relax the entire body, mind, and Spirit. A good meal, vitamins, tea, and then lots of sleep is in order. Sometimes you won't be able to sleep for several hours after you come down from a trip, because of the chemical still in your system. That's a good time to lie down and do self back-of-the-neck finger massage; cranial, and temple massage. An hour in this part of your head is well spent. An amazing amount of tension and pressure can be relieved in this way, and it resets your upper cranial electrical network. You'll be amazed how better you'll feel.

It's best to always store your acid in the freezer. Light, heat, & air degrade it. Keep it as impeccably fresh as possible.

Remember, a little goes a long way. **Low to moderately low doses favors amicable experiences.** One drop of liquid acid contains worlds of wisdom & wonder. That's how powerfully tiny this stuff is. Respect it. Never do more as you wait to get off on what you've already done. Be patient. Be prudent. Don't over dose.

The possibility of having a negative or bum trip, (or portion of a trip), is always present in the psychedelic experience. Most bummers are the result of being in the wrong environmental setting, feelings of nausea from not fasting or impure drugs, or a person's fears and insecurities rising to the surface and instead of being released, engulfing their consciousness in trauma, depression, or paranoia. It is best to let these feelings disperse upon arising, without congregating at the surface or overwhelming the mind.

Tripping is a self-revelatory experience, so oftentimes if a person is leading a life of false values, false goals, or an artificial ego, the psychedelic experience will reveal this to them, making them feel unsettled, distraught, and astray at their present state. This, however, is but the first step in the healing process; the initial realization and recognition of the problem... the first step towards the re-establishment of true direction. Just take this lesson in hand, think your way through, and let your thoughts progress to a different area. Recognize, but don't get stuck. Move on.

A person heading into a bummer can, on their own, edge back from the cliff and re-direct their thoughts and feelings to the positive mode. **Mood change is principally the key here. Mood change through thought change.** Once your thoughts move from their object of fear and disturbance, the mind becomes engaged in other areas of thinking and ceases to dwell on unpleasant perceptions. Changing the setting, Oming, deep breathing, and music, especially Beatles music, does wonders.

70

Be sure to both begin and end your Entheogenic journey in prayer; for the intricacy and beauty of this entire Cosmic Play is due to the One with the most vast imagination of all. Have trust and faith in the Creator, and fear shall know no home. If you do, however, become frightened or find uneasiness creeping within your train of thought, let it not. Just relax, sit down, shut your eyes, and breath deeply, distantly, and slowly. Follow your breath with your mind. Let the energy flow. Breathe deep the sea of silence, become the tranquil whole. Listen to the sounds of the forest. OM.

If you find yourself getting stuck on events or relationships of the past, release them with a laugh. Tears cleanse the Soul. The future holds your destiny, so meet tomorrow with an open heart.

Negative trips are totally controllable by one's own mind, and though they are rare on occurrence, the fact of their being should not stop the searcher from seeking, or knowing that they can be overcome by a change of environment, mood, music, thoughts, or positive inputs by others.

Occasionally a slight queasiness/uneasiness occurs as one initially begins to get off and the first fluttering of energy passes thru your body. This was referred to in my circles as the "High Speed Quibbles," and usually passes in 10-30 minutes once the lysergia fully kicks in.

In caring for someone who is in a negative psychedelic state, aptly called a bummer, remove them from the presence of people and external stimuli. Be kind, gentle, and smile a lot. Try deep breathing to calm them, and Oming to center them. Holding their hands will transfer your calming energy into them, and massage, (especially foot massage and very light circular temple massage, or massaging the temple & head's aura by not actually touching the head but keeping the hands 2-4 inches away), will bring them back into their body and out of their head. Mellow music will provide positive environmental stimuli which aids in mood change. Mental visualizations of objects, thoughts, people, animals, or landscapes will focus the person's attention in a different direction, and away from their pit of quicksand. Be supportive, talk gently, tell them stories, get them to laugh. Most of all be warm and positive in nature. You may have to go to the very edge or depths of Hell, pull them out, and bring them back. You can do it. I don't say this to scare you, but to prepare you. (In such cases, sitting opposite them cross-legged & holding their hands with eyes shut, is the way to go deep & retrieve one lost in the depths.) They'll be down in a few hours, so provide a warm positive environment & change the focus of their mind. **A person having a negative psychedelic experience should never be taken to the hospital; as their problem is not physical in nature, and the sterile and institutional environment of the hospital and its staff would only serve to bum them out further. The same definitely applies to psychiatric wards or police stations.**

In addition to lending calming, positive support to someone who is having a bad trip, it is also a good idea to neutralize the hallucinogen within the system. Vitamin B3, (niacin), chemically alters psychedelic substances, neutralizing their effects on the mind and body. Administering 1 gram/50 lbs. body weight will bring the person down in less than an hour. Niacin will temporarily cause the person to tingle, feel feverish, and become flushed, but this is a natural reaction and passes quickly. You could use niacinamide instead, which is buffered niacin and has none of the side effects mentioned but is not quite as readily effective as niacin. It may take a larger dose. Also effective, but not necessarily recommended, is 10-20 mg. of Valium.

As far as overdose goes, there is no chance whatsoever of physically overdosing on LSD, Peyote, Mushrooms, or Mescaline. What will occur if too much is taken, is that the subject's senses will become temporarily scrambled instead of heightened, leading to overwhelming feelings of bewilderment and confusion. If this occurs just relax, sit down, sit in Lotus position, or lie down and breath deeply and calmly for as long as it takes for clarity to return.

As far as Tryptamines goes, **a dosage of 5-MEO-DMT much larger than 6-10 mg. can have serious long-term psychological re-integration effects on the individual. This should never be done**. Measure precisely.   Many of the adverse effects of the use of hallucinogens were the result of the improper use of the substance, and a general ignorance of its true nature and scope... People taking too much at a time, impure substances, the paranoia brought on by the fact that the substance may be illegal, or the hospitalization or jailing of someone who was tripping in a misguided effort to help them, have all caused their share of bum trips in the past. Entheogens are nothing to fool with... if you're going to do them, know what you're doing.

<u>Low to moderate dosage & proper set & setting is the key</u>.

Currently in this country the use of psychedelics has been legislatively banned, with criminal penalties merely for their possession. The exception is peyote and the Native American Church, but the Sacramental use of Entheogens cannot be legislated or discriminated against according to creed or color. These are man's laws, not God's. For thousands of years psychoactive substances have been used by cultures in every part of the world for Spiritual and religious purposes, and remain so today. To legislate against them or the people that use them is religious persecution, and clearly an infringement of the basic religious freedoms as guaranteed by the Constitution of the United States. To worship God in the manner that you choose in privacy without any type of government interference, harassment, or sanctions, is our most Sacred and precious freedom. For the government to suggest otherwise through laws, penalization, etc. is morally corrupt and legally wrong, amounting to nothing more than a selective heretical Inquisition; on par with the tyrannical policies of the Dark Ages and Hitler's attempted extermination of the Jews, Gypsies, and the Jehova's Witnesses because of their religious preference and lifestyles.

Much of the reason that psychedelics are feared by governments is that they are in effect, intelligence drugs and de-programming tools. In the 60's, LSD had become the newfound pair of spectacles, before which the emperor and empire stood naked, seen for what they really were. And in a time of vast social injustice, an illegal & immoral war in which many of our friends, family, and selves were being killed, and the mass exploitation of the populace by the corporations who had considerable control over the government, (with their near-total control today), LSD was indeed a dangerous substance. The government would rather have us continue to be a nation of sheep, programmed & brainwashed by the lies of the Pentagon and the mindless drivel of television, than to become aware of the True nature their actions or the Divinity and power within us all that awaits to be awoken.

Certainly Entheogens must be used with care. That goes without question. Especially if they are tied to the yogic endeavor. But it cannot be denied that with proper use, psychedelics can offer a religious opportunity and experience of a depth and personal nature as few other experiences on Earth. Therefore, educate, don't legislate...

And remember, Jesus was illegal too...

It should be noted that four months after the first atomic fission was produced by the U.S. government in 1942, the psychoactive properties of LSD were discovered by the Swiss chemist Albert Hofmann. It is theorized that the discovery of LSD and the knowledge of its making was given to humankind at this point in our evolution in order to counter the very real threat that nuclear weapons represent to the human race, and indeed, to all life on Earth. Thus, along with the purpose of self-transcendence, Entheogens are meant to be used as a tool for developing self-awareness, and to raise human consciousness beyond the level of confrontational politics and self-annihilation, into an era of common concern and Peace for All.

"...Another reason for the incidence of religious experiences on LSD is the fact that the very core of the human mind is connected to God. This deepest root of our consciousness, which in the normal state is hidden by superficial activities of the mind, may become revealed by the action of the psychedelic drug.

Agreement exists among spiritual leaders that the continuation of the present development, characterized by increasing industrialization and overpopulation, will result in the exhaustion of natural resources and destroy the ecological basis for mankind's existence on this planet. This trend to self-annihilation is reinforced by international politics based on power trips and the preparation of weapons of apocalyptic potential.

This development can be stopped only by a change in the materialistic attitude that has caused this development. This change can result only from insight into the deepest spiritual roots of life and existence; an alteration of the consciousness of truth & reality that could be of evolutionary significance. LSD selectively and widely used, could be one means of helping the prepared mind become conscious of a deeper reality..."

Dr. Albert Hofmann Discoverer of LSD.
Author of LSD My Problem Child

MUSIC

If you employ Entheogens in your yogic attempt, then music can be a great aid in the endeavor. Since God's true form of existence- that of pure, vibrating, blissful, conscious energy is in essence the ultimate psychedelic state, then psychedelic music is the key. If you employ 5-MEO-DMT as the entheogen, music is not a requisite.

The 60's brought many spontaneous awakenings of Kundalini under the influence of LSD, dance, and Acid Rock. The vibratory rate of this music supersedes most, and resonates with the vibratory ascension, which is the yogic process. Certain songs lend themselves beautifully to be the musical backdrop for this Spiritual yogic unveiling. Music here serves the same purpose as mantra- raising the Soul's vibratory rate and aiding in activating the Kundalini through sonic intonation.

The following songs when played in order may well aid in your journey through Yoga. Again, this is merely knowledge that I have personally observed, and offer it only as such. A two hour soundtrack of Gregorian Chants or monks Oming may do just as well.

TRAFFIC- <u>John Barleycorn Must Die</u> *Glad*
Freedom Rider

BLIND FAITH- <u>Blind Faith</u> *Had to Cry Today*
In the Presence of the Lord
Can't Find My Way Home

BOB WEIR & KINGFISH- <u>Kingfish</u> *Lazy Lightning*
(Written about Kundalini.)

HOT TUNA- Double Dose *Serpent of Dreams*
(Written about Kundalini.)

THE BEATLES- Abbey Road

Come Together   *Mean Mr. Mustard*
Octopuses Garden   *She Came In Through*
I Want You   *The Bathroom Window*
Because   *Golden Slumbers*
You Never Give Me *Carry That Weight*
    Your Money   *The End*
Sun King   *Her Majesty*

JIMI HENDRIX- Electric Ladyland

And the Gods Made Love
Have You Ever Been To Electric Ladyland
Voodoo Chile
Rainy Day, Dream Away
1983
Turn the Tides Gently Away
All Along the Watchtower
Voodoo Chile Slight Return

JEFFERSON STARSHIP- Blows Against The Empire

Let's Go Together   *XM*
A Child Is Coming   *Starship*
Sunrise
Hijack
Have You Seen The Stars Tonight ?
This album is sonically designed to activate your Soul.

81

THE END

NOTES

1. In traditional yogic texts the Soul is said to be seated in the 7th chakra, or Sahasrara Chakra, called the seat of the Soul. The Kundalini is viewed as the feminine energy, Shakti; which is awoken at the base of the spine, led up the central canal of the spine to the Sahasrara Chakra where it unites with its male counterpart, the Shiva, releasing the Soul to return to Heaven.

In a major departure with tradition, I've defined the Kundalini Energy Itself as the Soul, residing in the Mooladhara Chakra at the base of the spine, needing to be awoken and led into and up the Sushumna to the Anja Chakra, (the 6th chakra the Pituitary Gland), where It unites with Consciousness and entering the Sahasara Chakra reaches the proper frequency & exits the body. This seems to me the simplest way to envision the process, and how I came to understand it based upon my first-hand experience. It may be technically incorrect according to ancient & Sacred tradition, but works perfectly nonetheless, and may indeed be easier to understand.

May the Masters forgive me for this deviation.

2. Complete knowledge of the process of Soul-release and Kundalini Yoga can be found exclusively in the personally researched & authenticated text-
Kundalini Yoga, Beyond the Cosmic Mirage.
A Manual for Self-Liberation
by Lewis Sanders.

This book can save you lifetimes on Earth.

87

BIBLIOGRAPHY

These reference books contain a wealth of excellent information for the Soul Seeker. Each and every one was lovingly and painstakingly done, and are outstanding in their field. They are monuments to what can be done with & within the mind. My gracious appreciation to the authors for those quotations from these books used in this manuscript for educational purposes. Thank You.

PHARMACOTHEON- Entheogenic drugs, their plant sources & history.
Jonathan Ott 1993
Natural Products Co
P.O. Box 1251
Occidental, Ca.
95465   (An essential read.)

TiHKAL:Tryptamines i Have Known And Loved-The Continuation.
Alexander & Ann Shulgin 1997
Transform Press
P.O. Box 13675
Berkeley, Ca.
94712

PSYCHEDELICS ENCYCLOPEDIA
Peter Stafford 1992
Ronin Publishing
Box 1035
Berkeley, Ca.
94701

THE ESSENTIAL PSYCHEDELIC GUIDE
D.M. Turner 1994
Panther Press
1032 Irving #514
San Francisco, Ca.
94122

LEGAL HIGHS
Adam Gotleib rev. 1992
20th Century Alchemist
P.O. Box 3684
Manhattan Beach, Ca.
90266

ENTHEOGENS AND THE FUTURE OF RELIGION
Council on Spiritual Practices 1997
Box 460065
San Francisco, Ca.
94146

THE SACRED RECORD
Official newsletter of
The Peyote Way Church of God
Star Route #1
Wilcox, Arizona 85643
The Peyote Way Church of God is
an awesome church to be a part of.

INTEGRAL HATHA YOGA
Swami Satchidananda; N.Y., 1970
Holt, Rinehart, & Winston

THE LIFE DIVINE
Sri Aurobindo; Sri Aurobinbo
Ashram Trust Pondicherry, India
An absolute classic on
Higher Consciousness.

KUNDALINI YOGA- BEYOND THE COSMIC MIRAGE.
A Manual for Self- Liberation
Lewis Sanders c 2019

THE SECRET OF THE GOLDEN FLOWER
Richard Wilhelm 1962
Mariner Books

THE QUEST OF THE GOLDEN STAIRS
Arthur E. Waite 1893. 1921
Theosophical Publishing House

PSYCHEDELIC PRAYERS
Timothy Leary 1966
Poet's Press

HIGH PRIEST
Timothy Leary 1968
New American Library

THE POLITICS OF ECSTASY
Timothy Leary 1968
Putnam

DISCLAIMER

This book is intended and provided for Truthful informational purposes only. Knowledge is the key to release. The publisher, author, & copyright holder do not advise or assume any responsibility for anything attempted beyond the reading. However it should be noted for the more than casual reader...
<u>All warnings herein should be strictly observed</u>.

OM SHANTI

Other Mind-Blowing Books by Lewis Sanders

WHAT A LONG STRANGE TRIP IT'S BEEN
A HIPPY'S HISTORY OF THE 60's & BEYOND...

DEAD DREAMS
UNDER ETERNITY WITH THE GRATEFUL DEAD.
A MYTHEOLOGICAL HISTORY

LYSERGIC INSURGENTS-
THE TRUE TALE OF WEIRD NORMAN
IN THE DAZE OF PSYCHEDELIA

KUNDALINI YOGA
BEYOND THE COSMIC MIRAGE.
A MANUAL FOR SELF-LIBERATION

THE GOLDEN CITY OF KUNDALINI

A SIMPLE GUIDE TO
HEALTH, HEALING, & DETOXIFICATION.
ALTERNATVE HEALING MODALITIES

ANTEDILUVIAN DEJA-VU.
THE COLLECTED POEMS OF LEWIS SANDERS

FEED YOUR HEAD

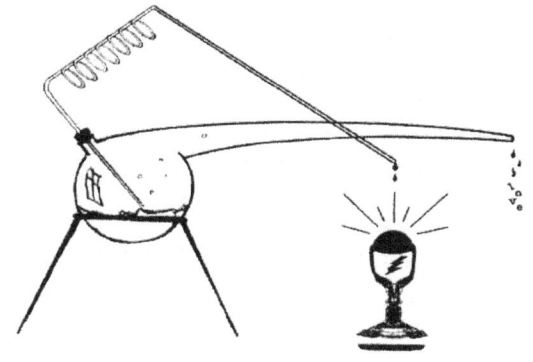

Eternity Blue Productions

Literary Distillations of Lysergic Proportions

Blow Your Mind From The Inside Out!

"Under Eternity...
        Under Eternity...
                Under Eternity Blue... "